Smells Like Rain

Smells Like Rain

Poems by
Gregory Luce

Sligo Creek Publishing Company

ISBN: 979-8-9911983-3-2

Sligo Creek Publishing Company
Silver Spring, Maryland
sligocreekpublishing.com

Cover Image by StockCake
Cover Design by Alan Abrams

For Sara and John

In memory of
Patricia D. and Warren W. Luce

Table of Contents

Subway Impromptu 1
End of Summer 2
Falling off the Earth 3
Black Coffee 4
Smells like rain 5
Tornado Year 6
From Anxiety Journal—Spring 2015 9
To S on Her Returning Home 12
Weldon Kees Walks to the Golden Gate 13
Poem for a New Year 14
No Escape 15
Ode to My Confederate Dead 16
River 18
On the Border 19
Through the Fumes of Whiskey 20
Into the Swamp 22
The Worm (Re)Turns 23
Winter Evening in Pioneer Square 24
Another Flight 25
Pharaoh Sanders Meets Coltrane in Heaven 26
Warm Canto 27
At Charlie Parker's Grave 29
Beginning With a Line From Jeff Buckley 30
Too Close 31
Tower 32
Acknowledgements 33
Bio 34

Subway Impromptu

Shrouded in a mantle of music
I ride the train, sleepy but open-eyed.
I pan my eyes around the car, take in
scenes of fellow passengers gesturing,
lips moving, a silent film with no title cards,
but an excellent soundtrack.

I am an eye in a camera in a phone,
taking in and storing images,
Laura Marling's voice soaring over all.

End of Summer

A sliver of moon
entangled in near-bare
branches trails a cloak
of cloud as crickets
chirr a last sonata
for summer
how many nights
like this in 61 years
the moon withdraws behind
the clouds but crickets
chorus on crescendo
diminuendo crescendo
how many times
have I written this poem
in the absence of moon
the night grows darker
as the wind scuds
the clouds along
how many more
nights like this.

Falling off the Earth

is easier than you might think
sit in a small room dark or
dimly lit and avoid
the window (remember Chet Baker)
remain inside and don't answer
the telephone you will fall
away or float up.

Black Coffee

She takes her coffee black
One half-teaspoon of sugar
precisely measured
she warms her hands
in the steam the aroma
takes her back
to a morning sitting
with her father
at the kitchen table
he takes his coffee black
gives her a sip
she makes a face
his laughter
when you're older
you'll like it
she looks outside
and wonders if
the clouds are made
of the steam
from all the coffee cups
in the world.

Smells like rain

he says and she
barely able to reach
his hand looks out
across the clear
sky at the thin
line along the far horizon.

Smells like rain
he says and she
taller now thinks
of rain slanting through
the wheat field ahead
of the Oklahoma wind
hearing him whisper please
Lord don't let it be hail.

Smells like rain
he says and she
taller still and with
a child of her own
looks at him shrunken
on the bed eyes half
open below his sweating
forehead his sister saying
open the window child
and the slightest breeze
ruffling his hair.
Smells like rain
he says and she
whispers smells like rain.

Tornado Year

That was the year
we almost lost everything,
he said.
You were, what, about 7?
Eight, she said,
I was in third grade.
And it'd rained all day,
he said, and then
the hail started
and I was praying
Not the wheat
Lord, not the wheat,
and then lightning hit
the barn and it goddamn
fell down smoking,
never seen such a thing,
and right then
your school bus
pulled up and the wheat
was getting smashed down....
The hail was hitting
the bus so hard, she said,
it sounded like we were
being shot at.
You looked so scared,
when you got off the bus
you were crying.
I wasn't scared,
I was crying because
the wind blew off
that stupid paper crown
I got for doing

the best drawing
of Snow White
and my hair was
getting soaked. I
never even saw....
You always did have
pretty hair just like
your mama. He blinked
and coughed.
Sorry, smoke.
He took another drag.
Your mama always
hated that I smoked these
things. I said to her
dang it, I don't drink
or play cards and
I don't hardly ever swear,
these things are all
I got. Anyways
you hadn't taken
two steps off the bus
when I just happened
to look up and them
clouds were spinning
and that goddamn
funnel dropped
heading straight
at the bus, it was all
happening so fast,
I was running like hell
to grab you and I was

saying Damn you, God,
first you took Ellie, and now
my wheat and my barn,
don't take my girl,
and the lightning hit
seemed like right behind me,
I could feel the jolt
and the little hairs
were standing up on my arms…

Me too, she said.
… and I thought, dang,
the next one's for me
but I grabbed you up
and run for the house,
and just like that it
all stopped, the sun
came out like nothing
happened.
He lit another cigarette.
As I recall, she said,
the next lightning strike
hit the steeple of
the First Baptist Church.
That's right, he said.
Y'know, your mama
always told me God
was a Methodist.

From **Anxiety Journal—Spring 2015**
(for John Huey, with profound gratitude)

"The mind is the cause of our distresses
but of it we can build anew."
                    —William Carlos Williams

I.
Write your way
out of it my friend said.
Can a ballpoint pen
cut through the mist nets
of dread that entangle
the heart and lungs
and tighten around
the temples?
Stand as a lightning rod
for the fevered currents that pulsate
along the nerves at four a.m.?
Provide the spark
that kickstarts paralyzed desire?
Will ink on paper
re-water the streams
where joy once flowed?

II.
Churchill's black dog
weighted his bed mornings,
rode his back for hours.
My caramel cat jumps
on and off the bed, noses
every box, rubs against
every piece of furniture,
cruises the windowsill
all through the dark hours
after midnight.

III.

"The Soul has Bandaged moments -
When too appalled to stir -
She feels some ghastly Fright come up
And stop to look at her"
                    —Emily Dickinson

When the net falls again
at 5 a.m. and wraps
the body tight at first,
then prickles over the skin
like a loose bandage
over a bloodless wound.

IV.

Living with nerve ends
a little too close
to the surface:
They vibrate
like steel strings
strummed with a razorblade.

V.

Tremor makes a partial rhyme
with *memory*. Text from
my sister: My great-aunt
died this morning.
Relief and *grief* make
a full rhyme.

VI.
A rare morning of equilibrium:
In a sunlit café
I look down 14th St.
COME UNTO ME
in giant red letters beckons
from the top of a building
but I'm not ready
to leave my seat
on the ground.

VII.
Breaking the surface
after almost drowning,
gulping air at first,
then easing into steady
rhythm of breath:
Shake the water
out of your hair,
float for a while.

To S on Her Returning Home

I. "The tulips are too excitable. It is winter here.
Look how white everything is, how quiet, how snowed in."
  —Sylvia Plath

First the unmarked snow, smooth, pure
under the low sky, then imprints, tracks,
drifts of leaves and paper, then the hard edges,
sharp ashy ridges crusted with dirt.
But finally a trickle of sun and then more
sun, flows of water, and patches of grass
astonishingly green.

II. "The soul has bandaged moments."
  —Emily Dickinson

The itch and sting, painful rustle, stick
and prickle, each breath measured out
like medicine, counted like gold coins
one on top of the other. The pain,
my surgeon said, that's the healing.

III. "The water I taste is warm and salt, like the sea,
And comes from a country as far away as health."
  —Sylvia Plath

Not for drinking but good for floating
until the strength to swim returns.
That country is on the far shore,
remote but attainable.

Weldon Kees Walks to the Golden Gate
"His sad and usual heart, dry as a winter leaf."
                    —Weldon Kees

Will a heart float
if detached from the body
that carries it? Is the heart
a rock or a balloon?
What happens when
the weight of the body
compresses around it?
How does it leap
into the throat? When
the heart sinks where
does it go? Do you still
have a heart to break?
Could you break it yourself
if you had to?

Poem for a New Year

The sun is aflame
above the Potomac
as the last shreds
of mist dissipate
above the shimmer
of the river's skin.
Bare branches along
the shore sparkle
with dewdrops
in the nascent air.
And I am poised
on the river's edge,
and I will fly
like the cormorant,
arrow-straight,
unswerving, upstream
toward the distant mountains.

No Escape

Take one if it hurts,
two if it doesn't
because the world is too much
it crowds in with its
traffic noise and cell phone
chatter, its birdsong, jazz
and guitar chords wafting
out of cafes, raindrops
spattering leaves,
its sunlight and unlit tunnels
its mobs on the Metro
and solitude in lonely parks
its jagged beauty and
encompassing horror

Take one if it hurts,
two if it doesn't
because I need to stay awake
and feel the pain and pleasure
and breathe however raggedly
equilibrium is critical
is everything right
speech right conduct
right effort now
abandon silence
exile cunning

Take one if it hurts,
two if it doesn't

Ode to My Confederate Dead

"Now that the salt of their blood/Stiffens the
saltier oblivion of the sea,/Seals the malignant
purity of the flood...."
> —Allen Tate

I don't own a Confederate flag—
no one, I think owns one, it owns them—
but I do have Confederate blood.
But what does that mean, blood?

Bloodlines: Do they tell in humans
the way they do in thoroughbreds?

Rivers and oceans of blood spilled for,
under, onto that flag, but some kept flowing
through one tiny channel down four generations
and ended up in my veins, blood that must mean
more than the slightly viscous liquid that circulates
in bodies and runs out red when the skin is cut,
for surely any Confederate blood I received at birth
has long since been replaced, not to mention diluted by
my father's cold Yankee blood, blood of small farmers,
sailors and whalers, merchants.

Blood carrying salt water, rocky soil, lumber,
iron ore.

But those two great-great-grandfathers in gray still march
somewhere back behind me and something connects them
to me so call it blood, call it Confederate blood, and what
does that mean and what do I do about it? Something tells
me the Black Lives Matter button on my favorite jacket
isn't quite enough....

If the salt of their blood has mixed so much and gone
to sea, if the flood—however malignant its purity—is
sealed,
perhaps it's time for one last look backward down the
bloodline
and then a letting go.

River

"Let us cross over the river and rest in the shade of the trees."—Stonewall Jackson's last words

Sorry, General, those trees have been
sold down the river for a cemetery
and your statue is going
to follow them, not the cargo
you fought to keep flowing,
nor the precious muscle
and bone you thought
you could own. Let the cotton
rot in the fields, the tobacco
desiccate and crumble, the wheels
fall off the wagons. Let the levees
collapse and the rivers—Tennessee,
Rappahannock, Missouri, Appomattox,
Potomac, Mississippi—overflow,
wash away the bloody stains.

On the Border
Frida Kahlo: "Self-Portrait on the Border
Between Mexico and the United States"

I stand astride the line between two worlds,
a bride in pink losing patience, my last
cigarette burning forgotten between the fingers
of my right hand. The sick sun, the sad moon,
the pink lightning cast a feeble light over
a Mexico turning gray, old temple
half gone and its stones gathered for
an unknown future. Even death is dead,
while the god and goddess stand as I do, defiant,
alone, forgotten as the lush flowers with deep roots
crowded into the corner.

Estados Unidos, your skyscrapers are rising higher
than your flag.
Estados Unidos, the smoke from Ford's factory is
beginning
to obscure your flag.
Estados Unidos, your welded pipelines are marching
across the land like the undead.
Estados Unidos, your electronics are putting deep roots
into your soil and connecting to our flowers.
Estados Unidos, I am waiting. Underground
the secret marriage has begun.

Through the Fumes of Whiskey

Like fallen powerlines
drifting in water her hair
floated toward my face
but stopped just short.
I started then froze.
She spoke:
Stop asking fools
for what you had and lost
back there in Texas.
I stared and sniffed
and caught the scent
of whiskey and another,
the smell of air after rain.
What are you wearing,
I asked, eau de bourbon
et l'air? A weak attempt,
but she smiled slightly
and went on. Texas
is Texas and everybody
is from somewhere and you
could get another drink.
She was right.
I was half drunk myself
and not getting there
fast enough. I found the bar.
When I turned around
she was right there.
I couldn't get past her,
so we sidled, a pair
of snakes trying to
emulate Astaire and Rogers,
toward a dark corner,
ice cubes tinkling like

broken keys in
accompaniment to our
jagged choreography.
What do you know
about me and Texas,
I asked. Her eyes
went vague. Oh,
you know, people
say things. I felt
a sudden chill
and thought someone
had opened a window.
Luckily the bourbon
was working and
rekindled some warmth.
She was looking off
toward another corner,
eyes half closed, maybe
trying to make someone out.
I have to go see—she
mumbled a name I couldn't
quite catch and faltered off.
I noticed her boots
for the first time.
Her right foot kept
slanting sideways
as she stumbled across
the room. I felt a bit
rickety myself. Home
or another whiskey?
I made my way haltingly
toward the bar.

Into the Swamp

The light is failing, Love,
and mist is slowly rising
from the bog with the last
birdcalls receding through
the pines. The emanation
of marsh gas may prick
our nostrils, Love,
but the rustle of cattails
counterpointed with
the plash of frogs
is sure to soothe.
Come, take my arm, Love,
and let us go gentle
into the tea-green twilight.

The Worm (Re)Turns

The Red-tailed hawk glides,
haughty, above the treetops,
sparring with ravens and crows.
Down in the canopy, gaudy
passerines sport and sing
among the leaves that flaunt
their verdant sheen. Far below,
the earthworm emerges, satisfied
with the work he has done.

Winter Evening in Pioneer Square

Murders of crows
and conspiracies of ravens
churn the evening sky
amid flurries of crystalline
snowflakes. Such murmurations
as I have never witnessed
and I stand transfixed, cold
feet forgotten, honks, caws,
and clacks swirling among
the icy diamonds glittering
the dark blue air.

Another Flight

Moving imperceptibly through
the world above the clouds,
which is no world at all
but pure ether, time
between cities attenuated
to fine fiber along which
we glide. Cut from
our tether to earth
we seem to float,
superior briefly even
to birds, until gravity
reasserts its rule
the plane sinks as
the heart rises in
the chest and we
bump along the earth
once more.

Pharaoh Sanders Meets Coltrane in Heaven

You built the stairway
I just followed the light
and tried to add more stairs
I saw the end of the line
you left hanging in the air
and reached always reached
to grasp it always reaching
I left the end hanging
for the next one to reach

Warm Canto
(Mal Waldron, Eric Dolphy, Ron Carter)

for Emily

She reminded me of you,
sitting there in front of
the coffeeshop—a bit taller,
maybe a bit older—still,
composed, a small spark
in the deep blue eyes,
gazing straight ahead
at a point somewhere between
my left shoulder and one hundred
miles away.

I hadn't thought of you
for months but your face appeared
now, looking down, half-smiling
and slightly sideways, your eyes shy
with just a glint of élan. Suddenly
the street noise diminished.
Dolphy's clarinet notes floated
gently above Waldron's light-
stepped fingerings in the air
behind my head.

You slipped away abruptly,
emailing goodbye. I had
no hold on you, neither
father nor lover, but you left
a little fissure in my chest
which throbs occasionally
when I see or hear something
that reminds me of you like
now as I tried not to stare,
still hearing Waldron now
in step with Ron Carter's
fingers plucking their way
down the cello's neck.

At Charlie Parker's Grave
(for Gregg Ottinger)

We stood there and I played
a few phrases of "Ornithology"
on my phone, while birds
were singing in the trees
and bushes and making
their presence known
with little percussive
rustles and chirps.
The sky over Kansas City
was clear and blue,
like Bird's blowing
on "All the Things You Are."
I gazed in silence and
was about to turn away
when I took another look,
saw the other marker, Addie
Parker, the mother who
raised him, who denied
him nothing, who bought
him his first saxophone,
in whose eyes he could
do no wrong, and who,
outlived him by 12 years
My friend said a few words,
we dropped some wild violets—
the only flowers at hand—
on both markers, and stepped
quietly away.

Beginning With a Line From Jeff Buckley

My kingdom for a kiss
upon her shoulder. She dances
always just at the limit
of vision, not dancing really,
stepping lightly along
the wavering horizon, shimmering
with last sun or early starlight,
she continually recedes yet
always remains, moving.
I can see her eyes, lit up,
gazing in my direction,
though whether she sees me
I can't say. If I close my eyes,
she's gone when I open them again.
She'll come back tomorrow,
always beyond my fingers.
I have no kingdom.

Too Close
(after Heisenberg)

The way when you look
too close you don't see
everything clearly when
you look right into your lover's
eyes and can't see the pain
plus he's good at hiding it
anyway and he looks back
and can't see the history
that comes alive every time
he raises his voice
plus you don't talk
about it anyway
as autopsies say
no visible marks or scars
not even a birthmark
they get embedded later
and very deep.

Tower
for Naomi

I don't know why I let you into the tower in the first place.
I don't know why I let you come all the way up.
I don't know why you wanted to.
I don't know why I let you open the windows and turn on
more light.
I don't know why I let myself go out into the day and night,
the sun and rain with you.
I don't know why my Fortress of Solitude became less
solitary.
I don't know why it seemed larger when you were there.
I don't know why you stayed when I tried to weave myself
into a cocoon.
I don't know why I let you help me tear myself back out.

I know the air up there started to seem a little thin.
I know the walls seemed to start to constrict.
I know I breathe easier outside with you.
I know the tower is crumbling.

Let's watch it fall.

Acknowledgements

"From Anxiety Journal"—Spring 2015," "To S on Her Returning Home," were published in *Deaf Poets Society,* Issue 1, August 2016.

The following poems appeared on *What Rough Beast:* "Ode to My Confederate Dead," *April 29, 2017;* "Too Close," *May 25, 2018*; "Weldon Kees Walks to the Golden Gate," *July 10, 2019;* "Not the Wolf," *December 9, 2019.*

"Another Flight," was published in *Broadkill Review,* November-December 2017.

"No Escape" was published in *Mile Nine,* February 14, 2019
"Through the Fumes of Whiskey" appeared in *Rye Whiskey Review.*

"Black Coffee" appeared on *Coffee Labs POM, March 2020*

"Smells Like Rain" was published in *Gargoyle, Issue #73.*

"Tornado Year" and "Into the Swamp" were published in *The Dead Mule School of Southern Literature, July 2020*

"Pharoah Sanders Meets Coltrane in Heaven" was published in *Gargoyle Online, January 2023*

"River" appeared in *Wordpeace*, March 2023

"Warm Canto" and "At Charlie Parker's Grave" were published in *Jerry Jazz Review, January 2024*

Photo by Matthew Bailey

Bio

Gregory Luce was born in Dallas, Texas, and grew up in Texas, Kentucky and Oklahoma. He holds a BA and MA from Oklahoma State University and did additional graduate work at the University of Southern Mississippi. He lives in Arlington, VA.

Gregory Luce is the author of *Signs of Small Grace, Drinking Weather, Tile,* and *Riffs & Improvisations.* His poems have appeared in numerous print and online journals and in the anthologies *Living in Storms* (Eastern Washington University Press), *Written in Arlington* (Paycock Press), and *This Is What America Looks Like* (Washington Writers Publishing House).

In 2014, he was awarded the Larry Neal Award for adult poetry by the D.C. Commission on the Arts and Humanities. In addition to poetry, he writes a monthly column for the online art journal *Scene4.*

www.ingramcontent.com/pod-product-compliance
Lightning Source LLC
Chambersburg PA
CBHW070453130626
46553CB00006B/2394